• • CASE SIZE • •

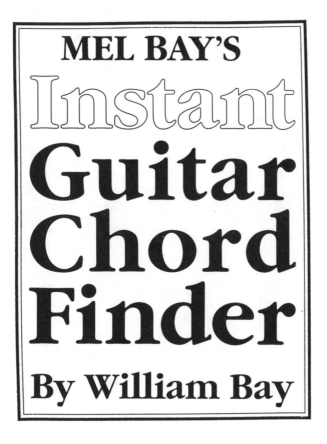

MEL BAY'S
Instant
Guitar
Chord
Finder
By William Bay

D0187960

Contents

How to Read the Diagrams

Each diagram is like a road map. Here is what the various symbols represent:

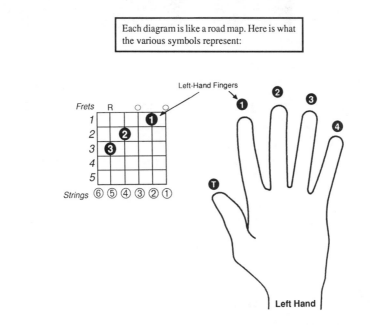

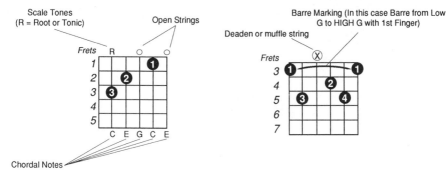

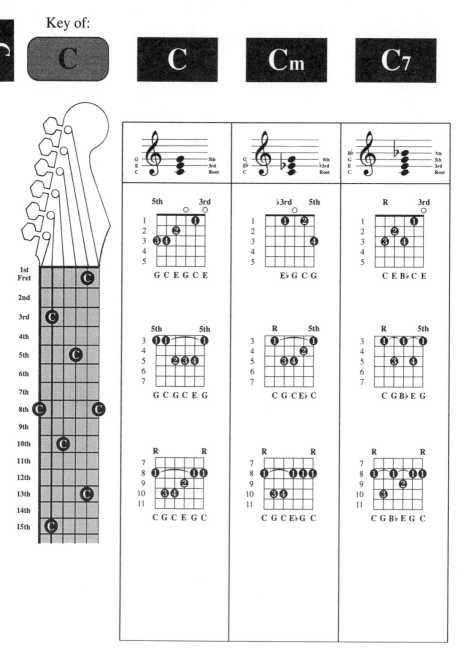

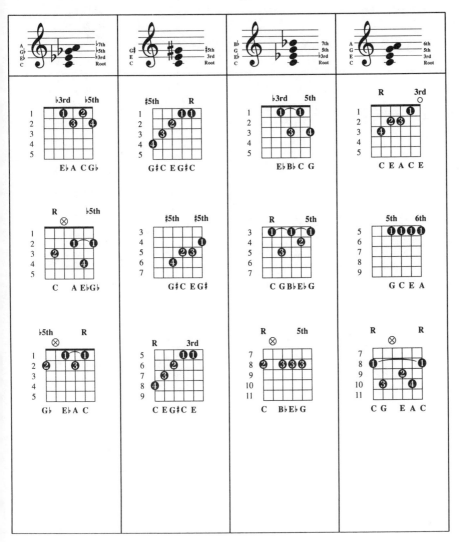

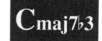

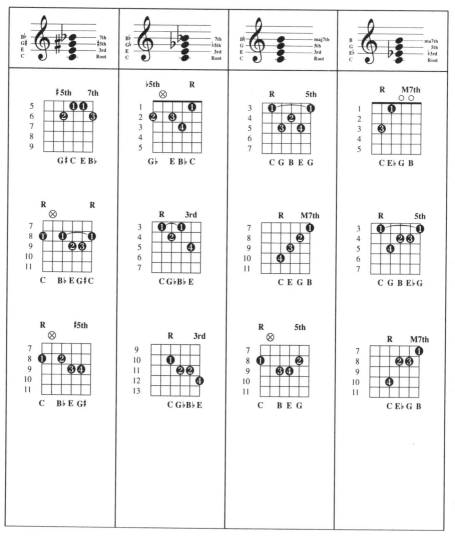

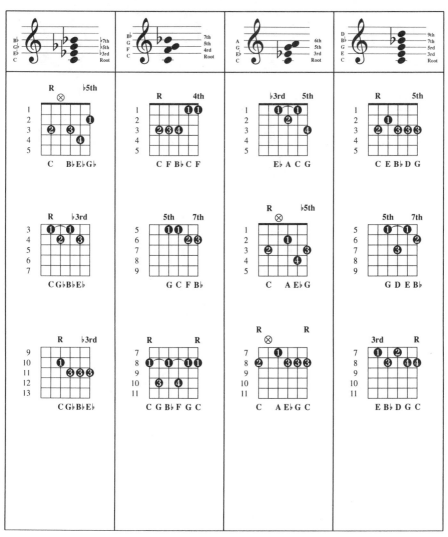

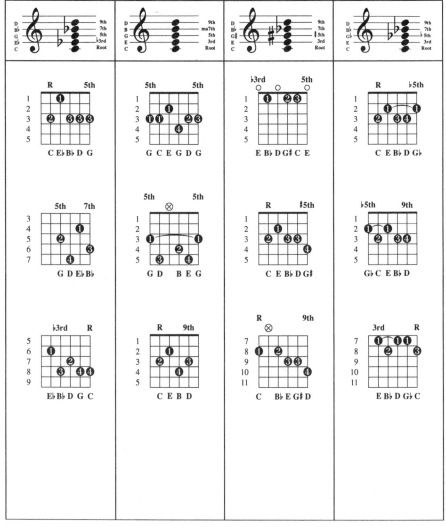

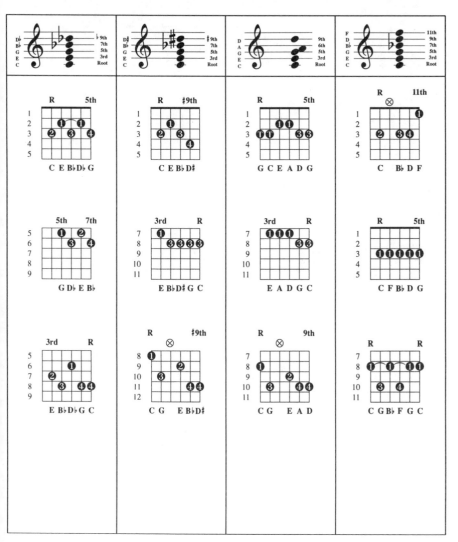

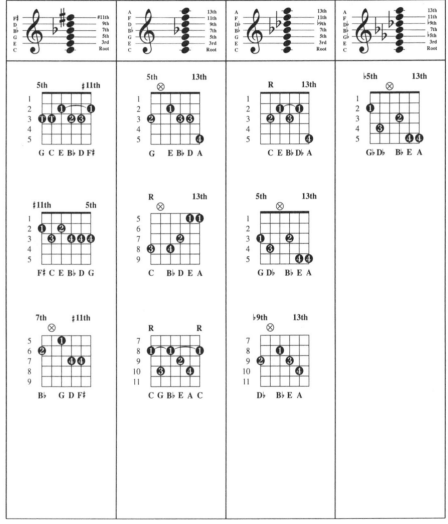

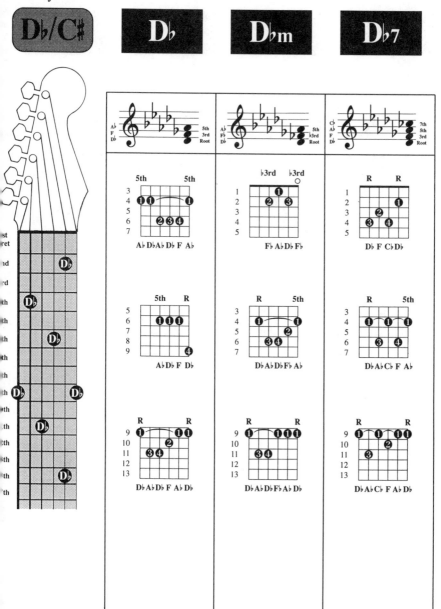

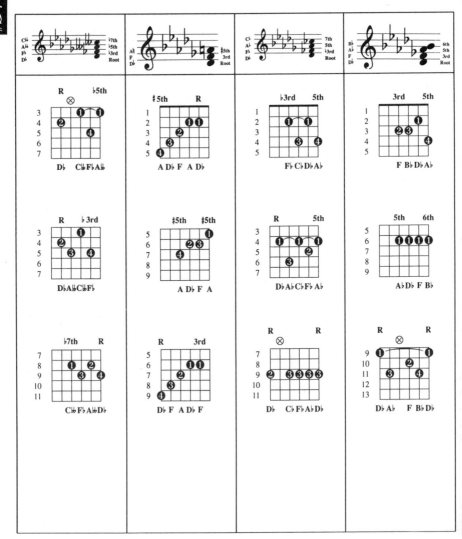

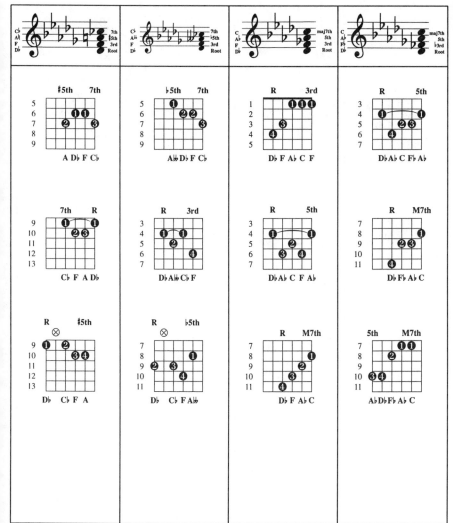

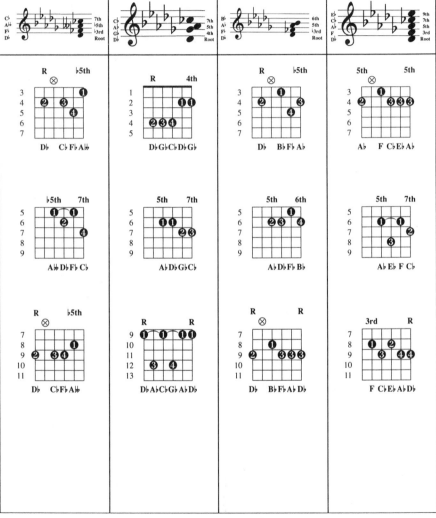

Db/C#

Dbm9

Staff notes: Eb / Cb / Ab / Fb / Db — 9th, 7th, 5th, b3rd, Root

Position 1 (frets 1–5): b3rd, 5th
- Fb Cb Eb Ab

Position 2 (frets 7–11): b3rd, R
- Fb Cb Eb Ab Db

Position 3 (frets 9–13): 7th, 9th
- Cb Fb Ab Eb

Dbmaj9

Staff notes: Eb / C / Ab / F / Db — 9th, maj7th, 5th, 3rd, Root

Position 1 (frets 1–5): R, 3rd
- Db Eb Ab C F

Position 2 (frets 3–7): 5th, 5th ⊗
- Ab Eb C FAb

Position 3 (frets 5–9): 5th, M7th
- Ab Eb F C

Db9+5

Staff notes: Eb / Cb / Ab / F / Db — 9th, b7th, #5th, 3rd, Root

Position 1 (frets 1–5): 7th, 3rd
- Cb Eb A Db F

Position 2 (frets 3–7): R, #5th
- Db F Cb Eb A

Position 3 (frets 9–13): R ⊗, 9th
- Db Cb F A Eb

Db9-5

Staff notes: Eb / Cb / Abb / F / Db — 9th, 7th, b5th, 3rd, Root

Position 1 (frets 3–7): R, b5th
- Db F Cb Eb Abb

Position 2 (frets 3–7): b5th, 9th ⊗
- Abb F Cb Eb

Position 3 (frets 7–11): 3rd, R
- F Cb Eb Abb Db

17

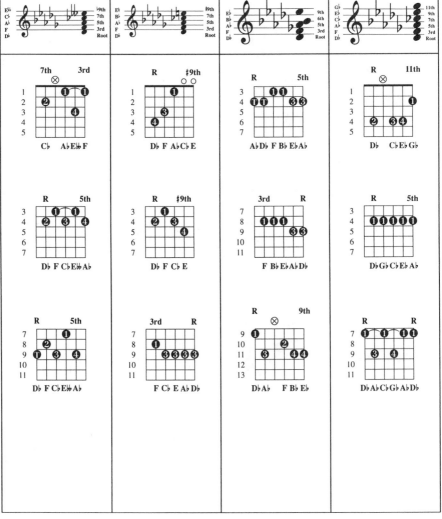

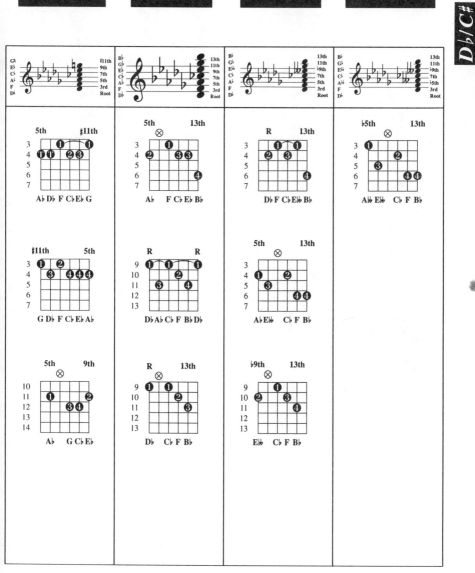

19

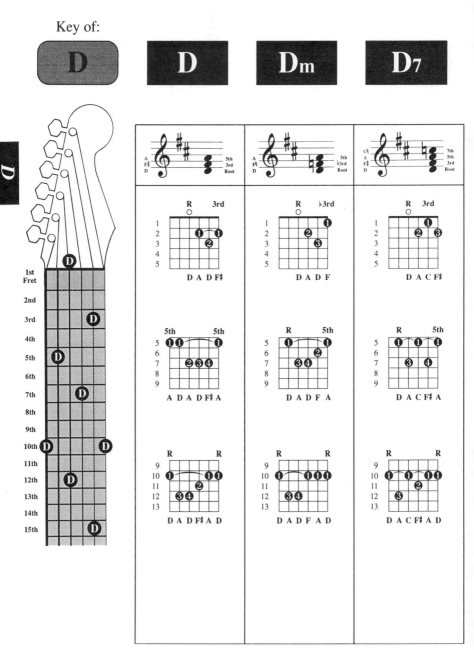

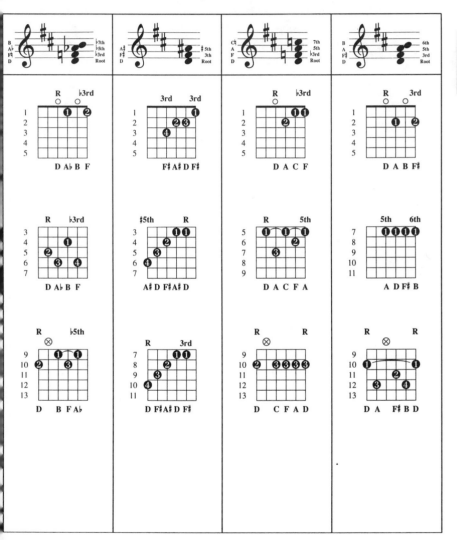

21

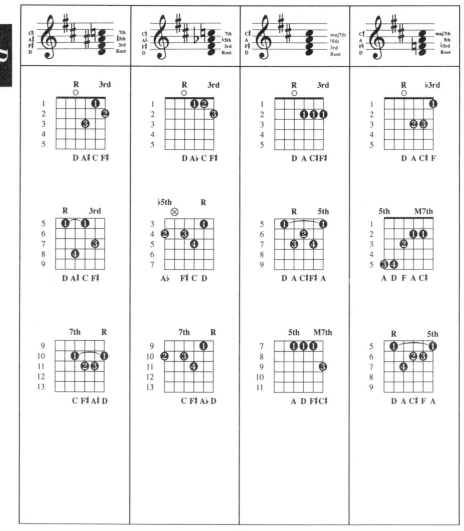

Dm7♭5　 **D7sus4**　 **Dm6**　 **D9**

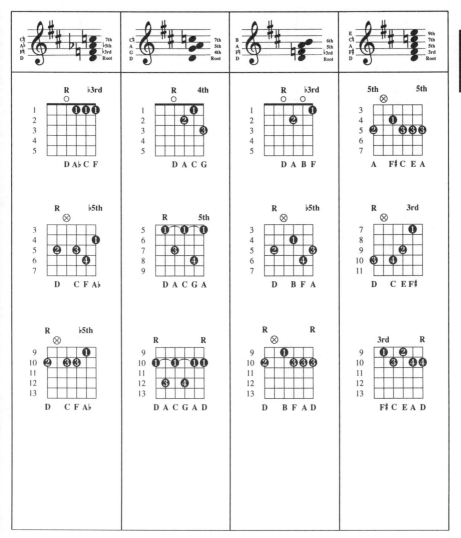

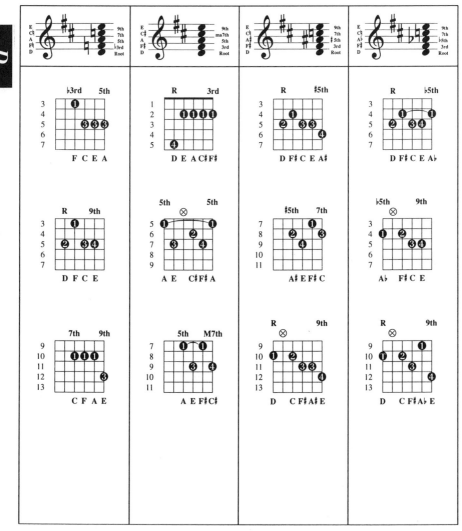

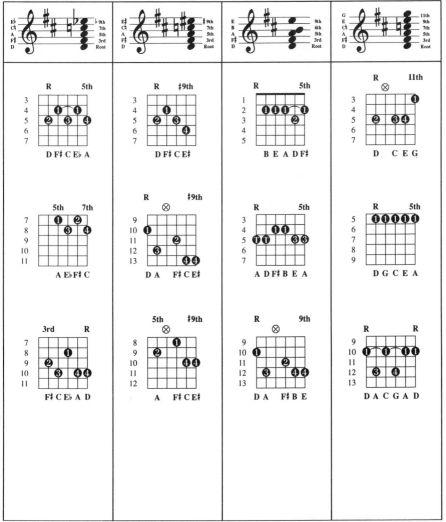

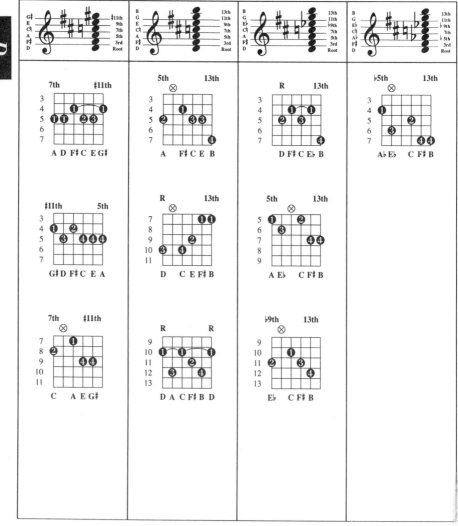

Key of:

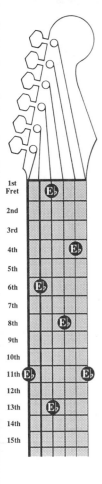

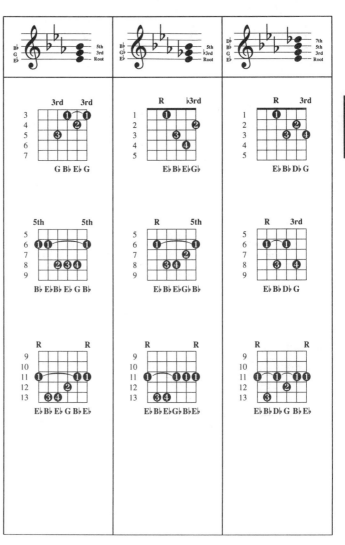

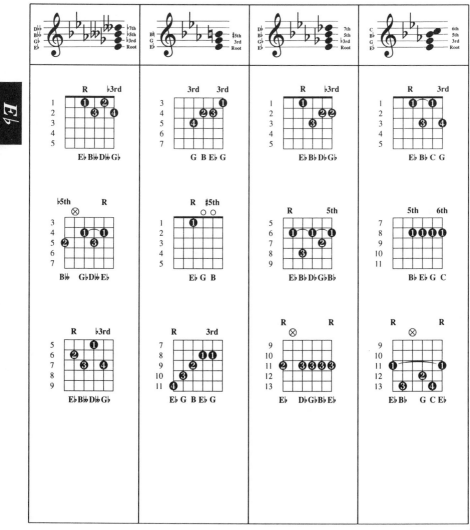

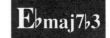

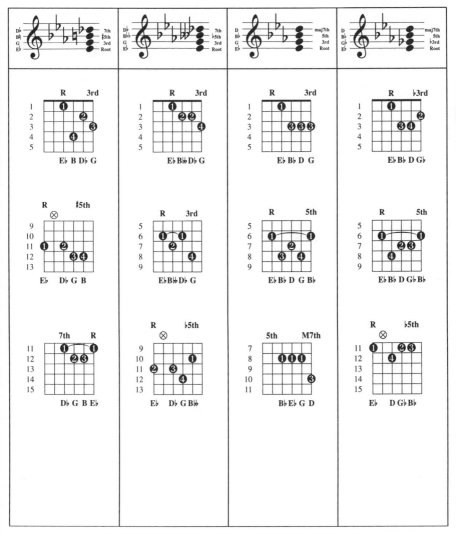

29

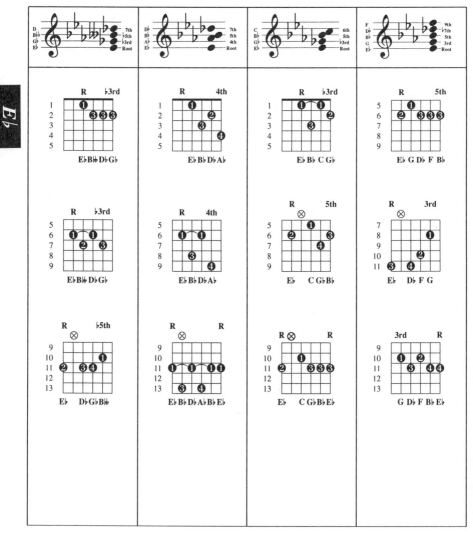

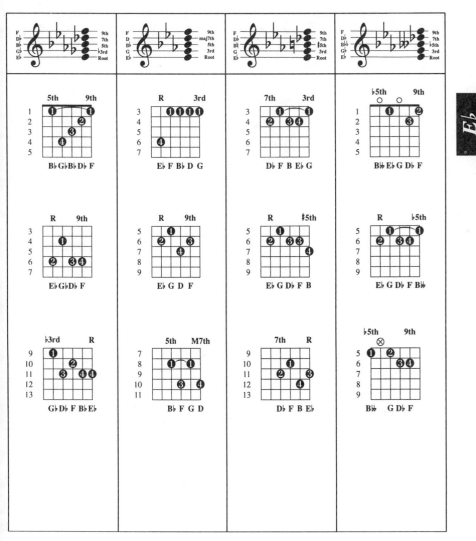

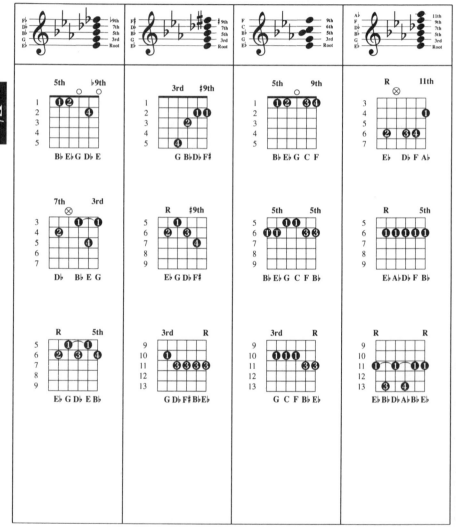

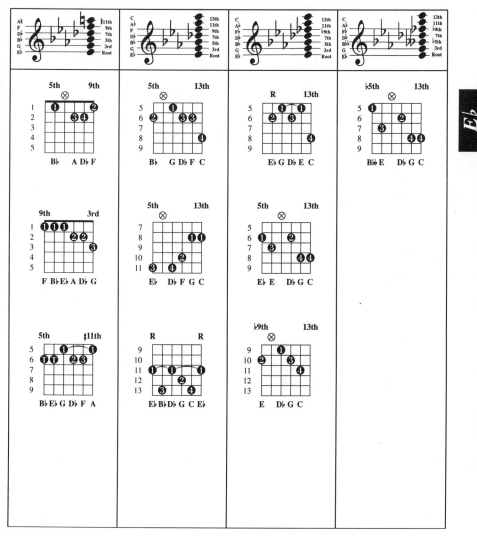

33

Key of:

E

E

Em

E7

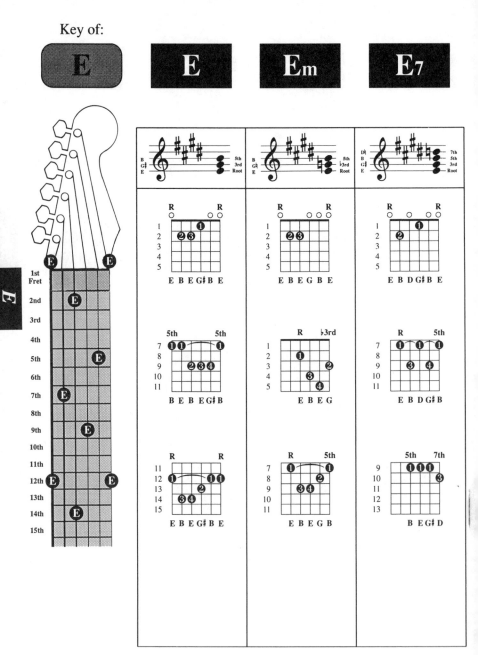

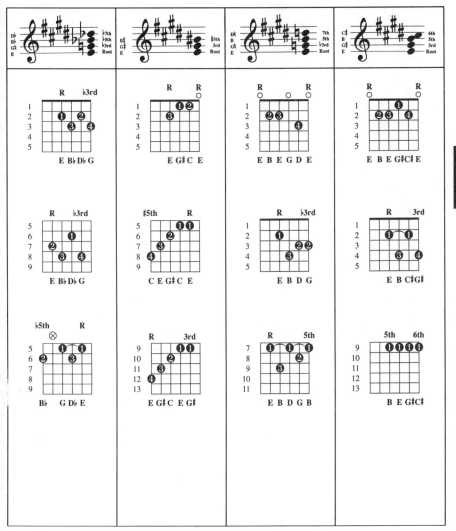

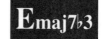

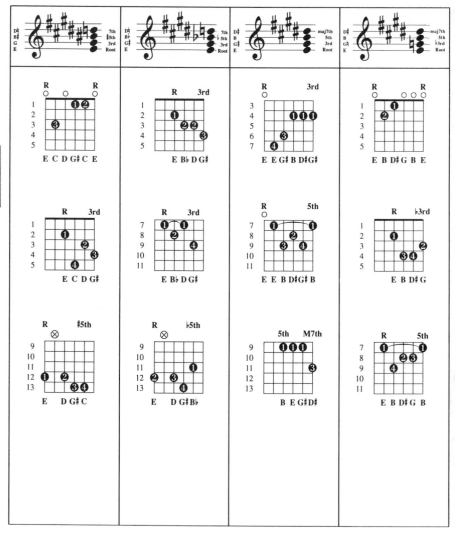

Em7♭5 E7sus4 Em6 E9

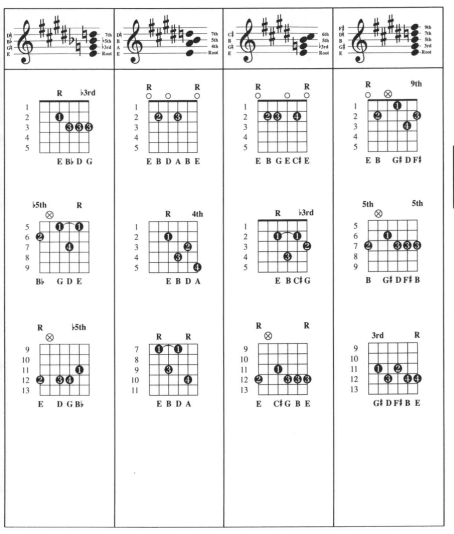

37

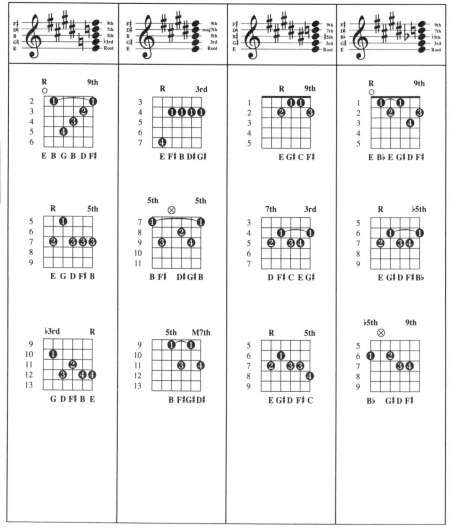

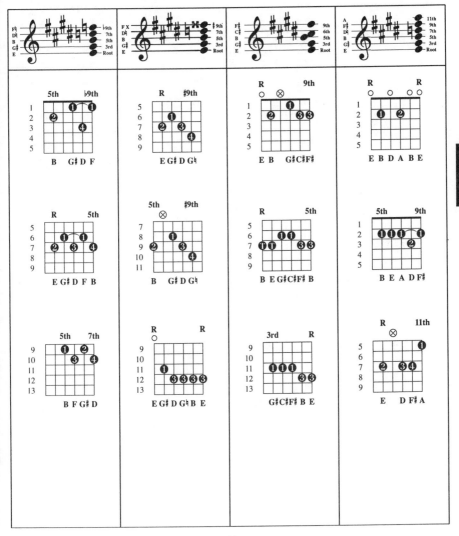

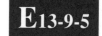

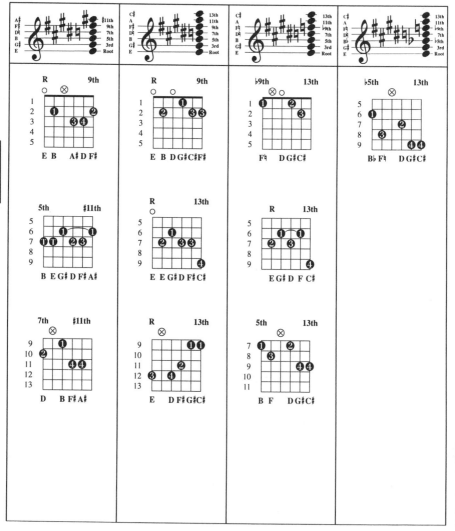

Key of: **F**

F   **F**   **Fm**   **F7**

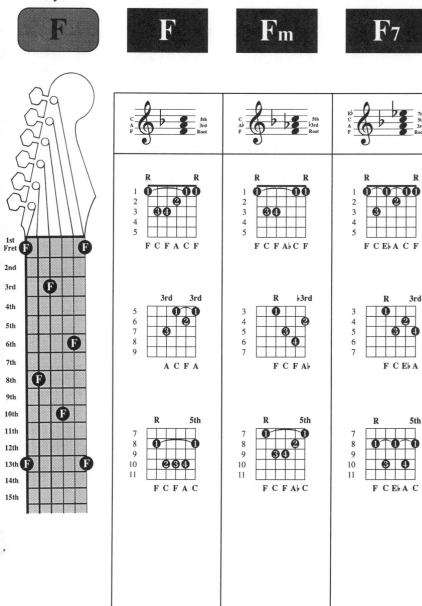

Fretboard (left side)

1st Fret	F ... F
2nd	
3rd	F
4th	
5th	
6th	F
7th	
8th	F
9th	
10th	F
11th	
12th	
13th	F ... F
14th	
15th	

F

Notation: C (5th), A (3rd), F (Root)

R ... **R**
```
1  ● ●●●
2      ②
3    ❸❹
4
5
```
F C F A C F

3rd ... **3rd**
```
5  ● ●
6     ②
7  ❸
8
9
```
A C F A

R ... **5th**
```
7
8  ● ●
9
10  ❷❸❹
11
```
F C F A C

Fm

Notation: C (5th), A♭ (♭3rd), F (Root)

R ... **R**
```
1  ● ●●
2
3    ❸❹
4
5
```
F C F A♭ C F

R ... **♭3rd**
```
3  ●
4      ②
5    ❸
6        ❹
7
```
F C F A♭

R ... **5th**
```
7  ● ●
8      ②
9  ❸❹
10
11
```
F C F A♭ C

F7

Notation: E♭, C, A, F (7th), (5th), (3rd), (Root)

R ... **R**
```
1  ● ●●●
2      ②
3    ❸
4
5
```
F C E♭ A C F

R ... **3rd**
```
3  ●
4      ②
5    ❸  ❹
6
7
```
F C E♭ A

R ... **5th**
```
7
8  ● ● ●
9
10   ❸  ❹
11
```
F C E♭ A C

41

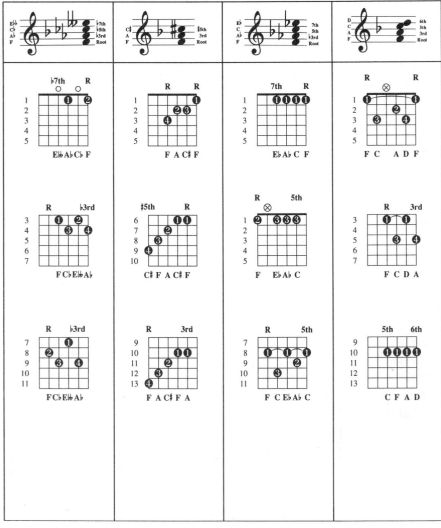

42

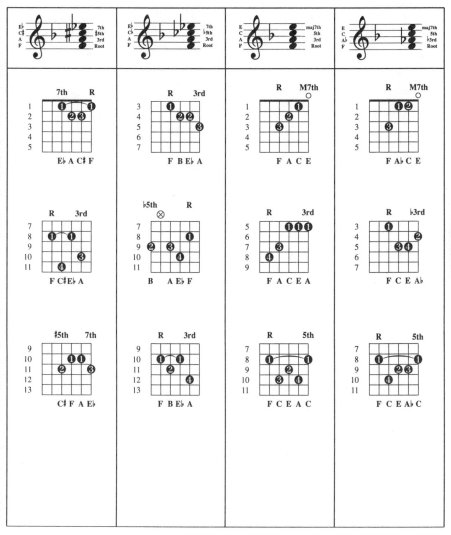

43

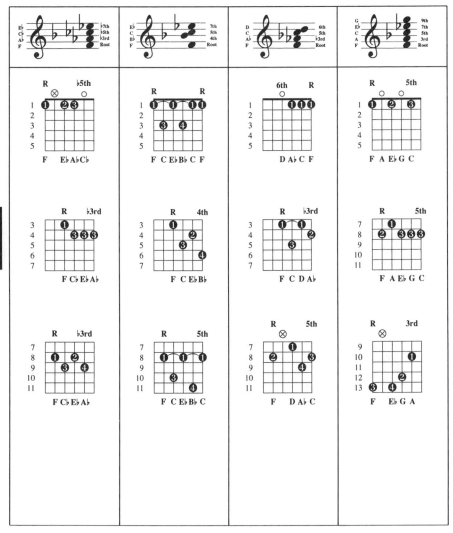

44

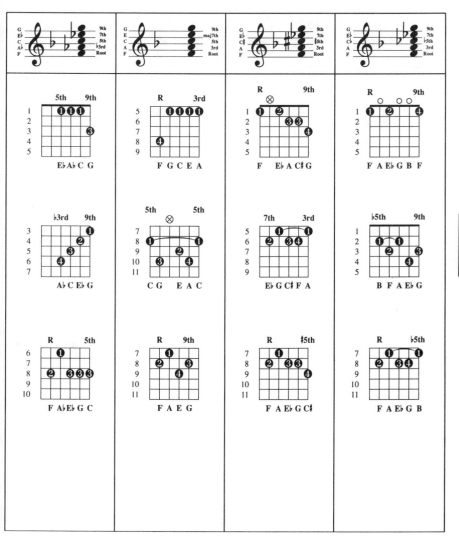

45

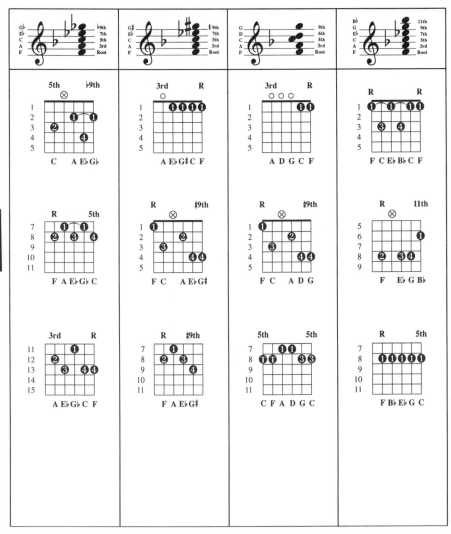

46

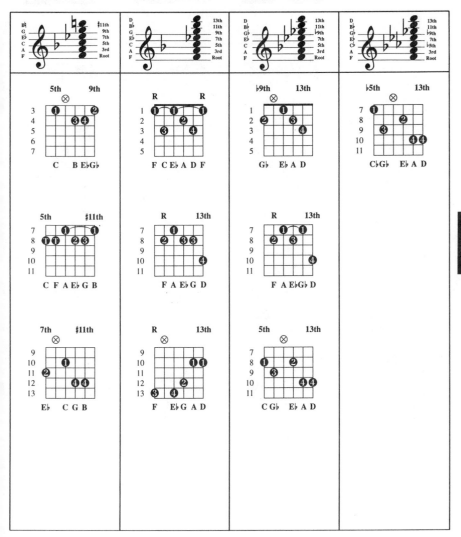

47

Key of:

F#/Gb

F#/Gb

F#m/Gbm

F#7/Gb7

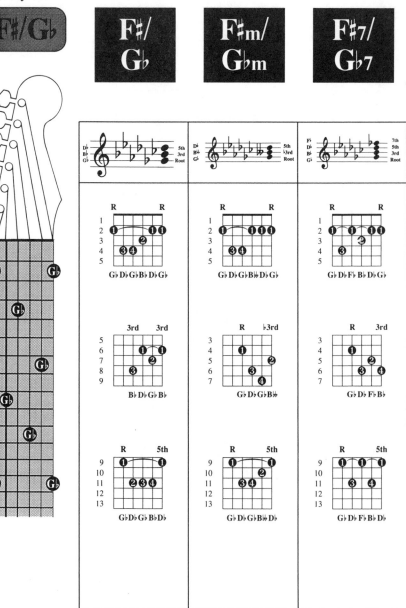

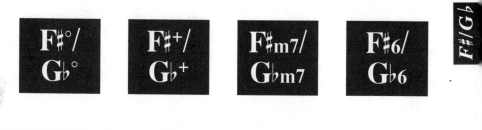

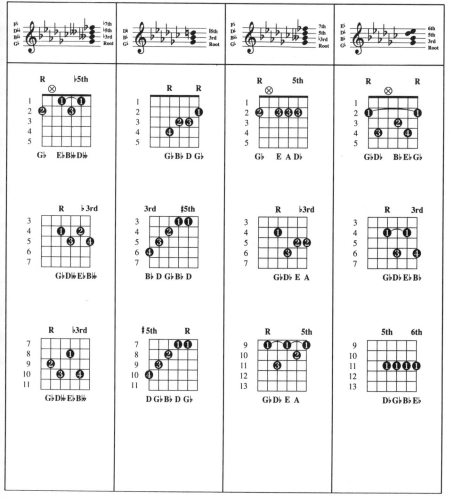

49

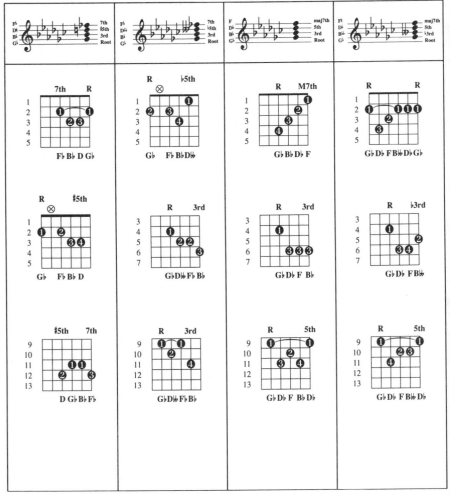

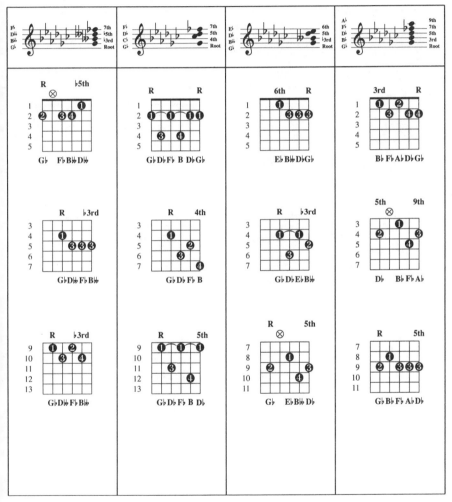

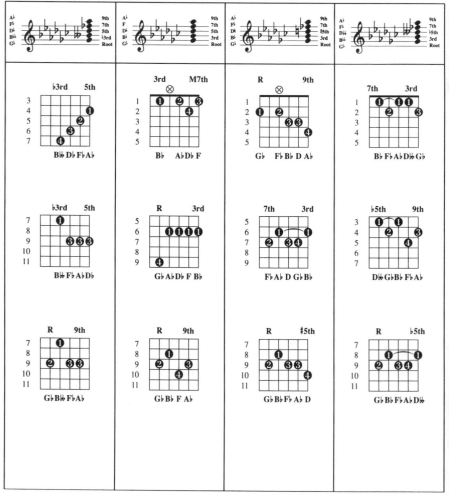

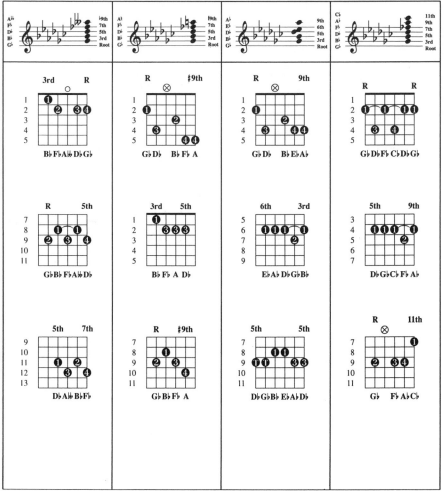

53

F#aug11/ Gbaug11

F#13/ Gb13

F#13-9/ Gb13-9

F#13-9-5/ Gb13-9-5

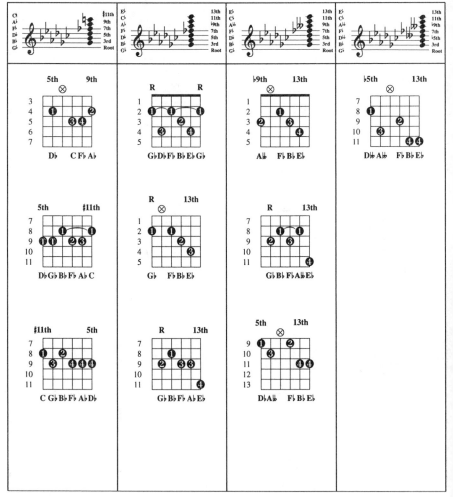

Key of:

G

G   Gm   G₇

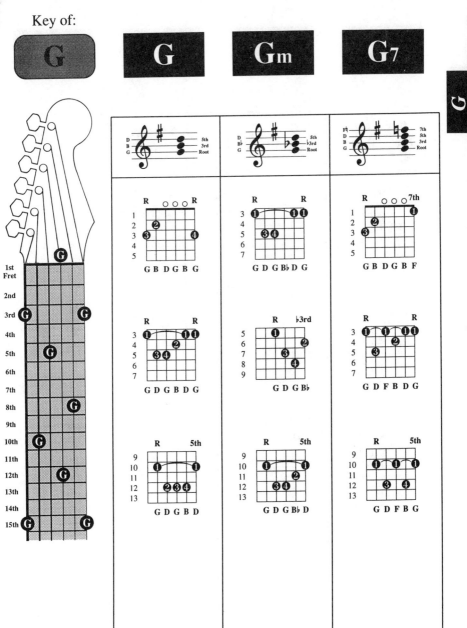

G chord positions:
- R ○ ○ ○ R — frets 1–5, fingers 2,3,4 — G B D G B G
- R ... R — frets 3–7, finger 1,2,3,4 — G D G B D G
- R ... 5th — frets 9–13 — G D G B D

Gm chord positions:
- R ... R — frets 3–7 — G D G B♭ D G
- R ... ♭3rd — frets 5–9 — G D G B♭
- R ... 5th — frets 9–13 — G D G B♭ D

G₇ chord positions:
- R ○ ○ ○ 7th — frets 1–5 — G B D G B F
- R ... R — frets 3–7 — G D F B D G
- R ... 5th — frets 9–13 — G D F B G

55

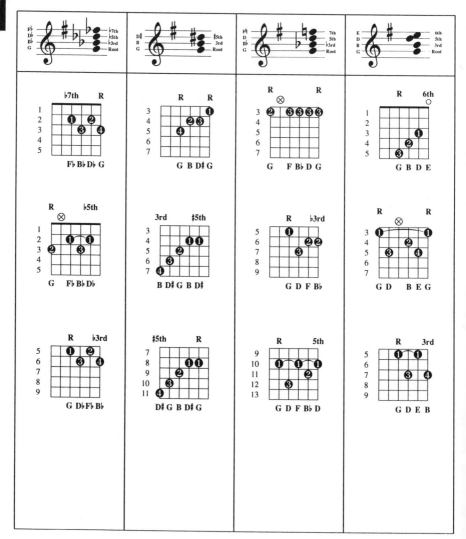

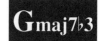

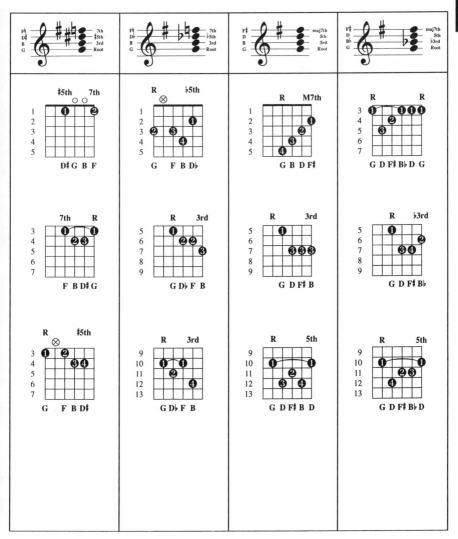

57

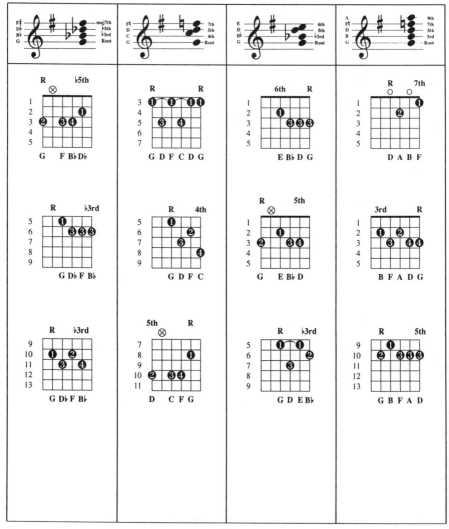

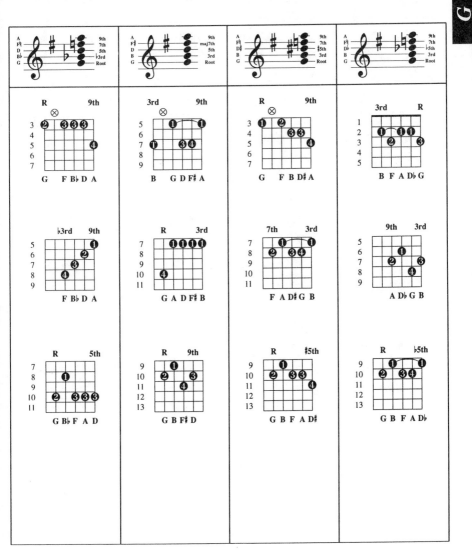

G7-9	G7#9	G6 9	G11

G7-9

Notation: Ab, F#, D, B, G — b9th, 7th, 5th, 3rd, Root

3rd — R
1 2 3 4 5
B F Ab D G

7th — b9th
3 4 5 6 7
F B D Ab

R — 5th
9 10 11 12 13
G B F Ab D

G7#9

Notation: A#, F#, D, B, G — #9th, 7th, 5th, 3rd, Root

3rd — 5th
1 2 3 4 5
B F A# D

R — #9th ⊗
3 4 5 6 7
G D   B F A#

R — #9th
9 10 11 12 13
G B F A#

G6 9

Notation: A, E, D, B, G — 9th, 6th, 5th, 3rd, Root

R — R
1 2 3 4 5
B E A D G

R — 9th ⊗
3 4 5 6 7
G D   B E A

5th — 5th
9 10 11 12 13
D G B E A D

G11

Notation: C, A, F#, D, B, G — 11th, 9th, 7th, 5th, 3rd, Root

R — R
3 4 5 6 7
G D F C D G

R — 11th ⊗
7 8 9 10 11
G   F A C

R — 5th
9 10 11 12 13
G C F A D

60

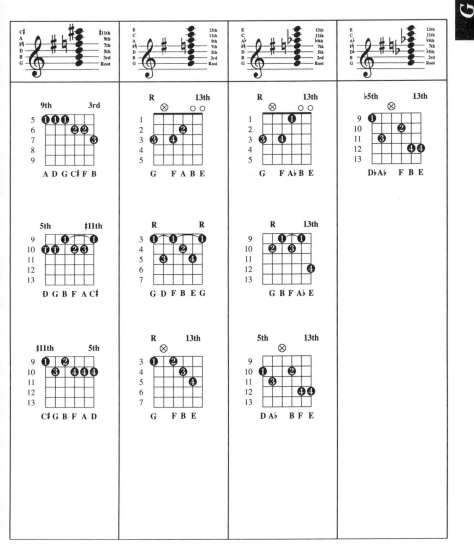

Key of:

G♯/A♭

G♯/A♭   **G♯m/A♭m**   **G♯7/A♭7**

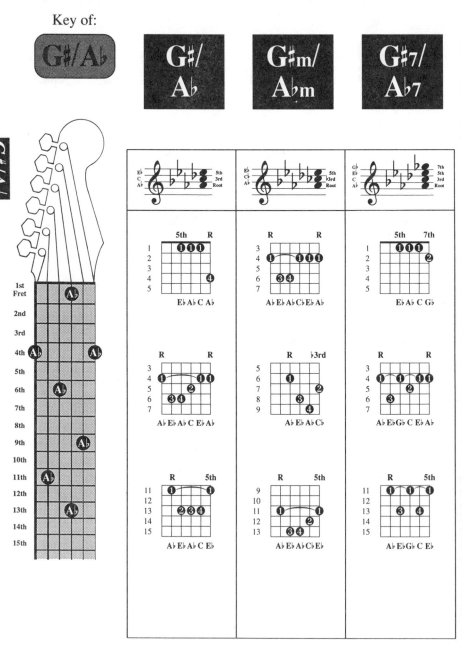

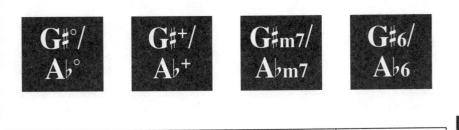

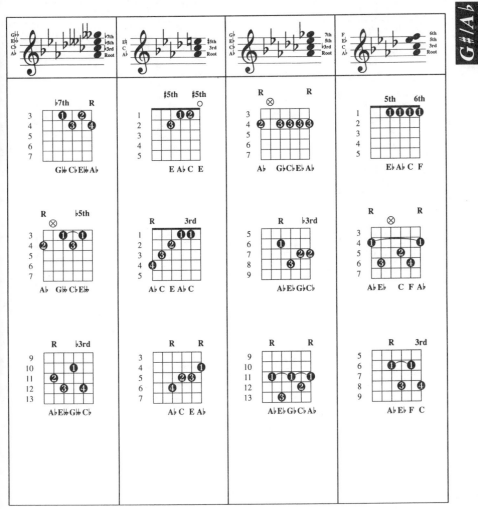

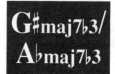

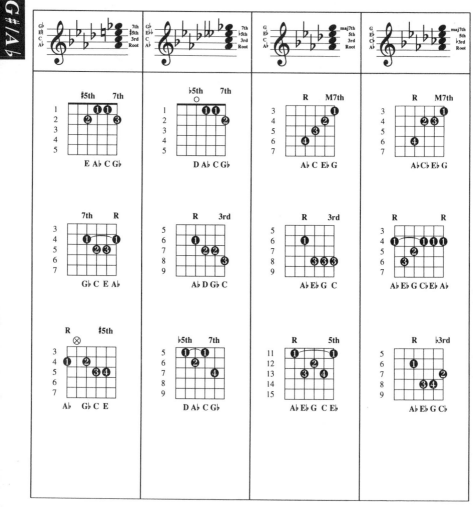

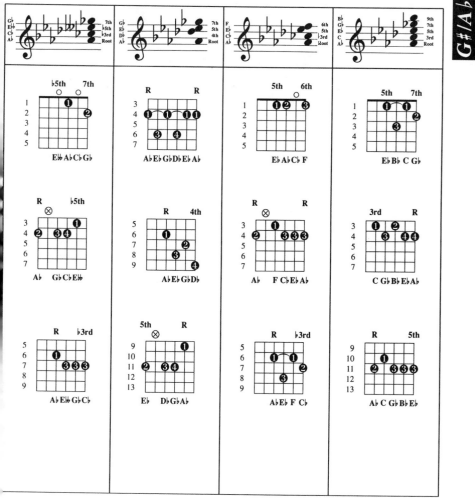

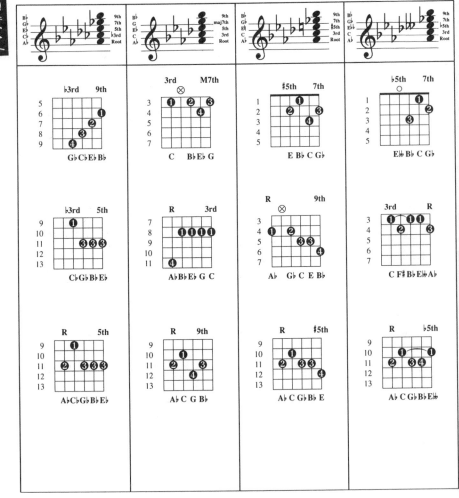

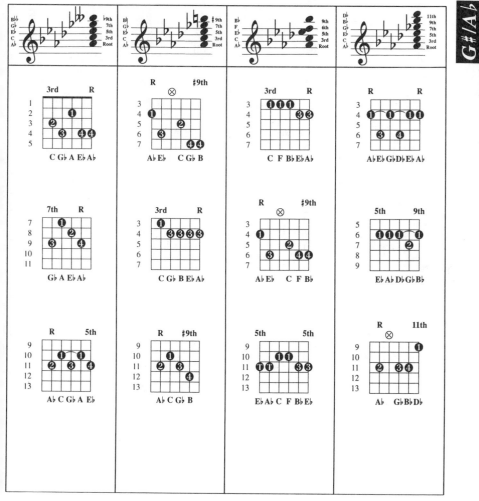

   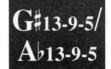

G#/Ab

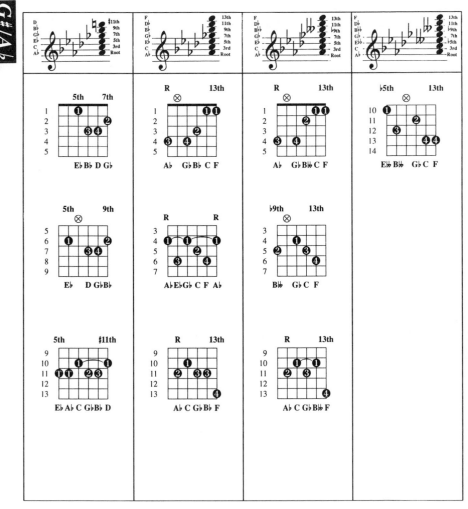

Key of:

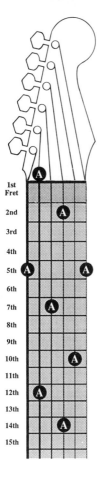
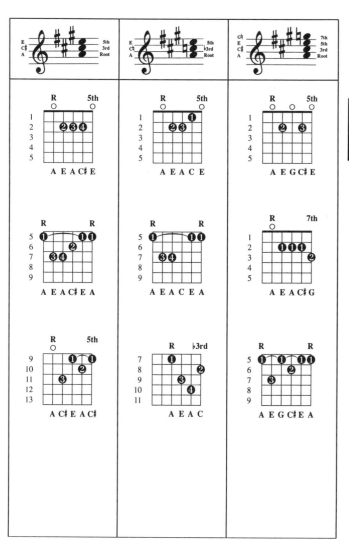

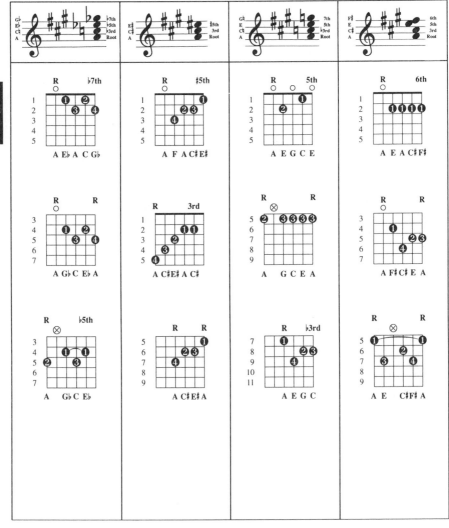

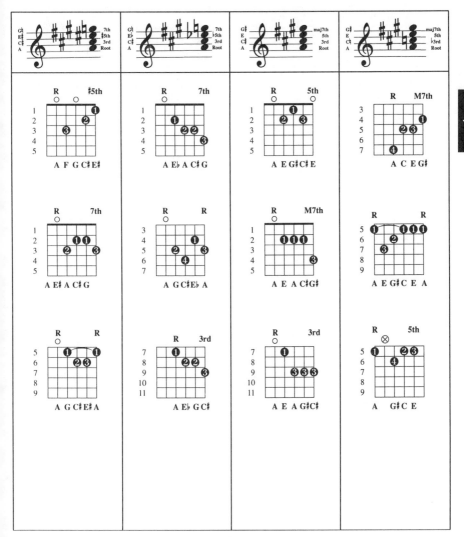

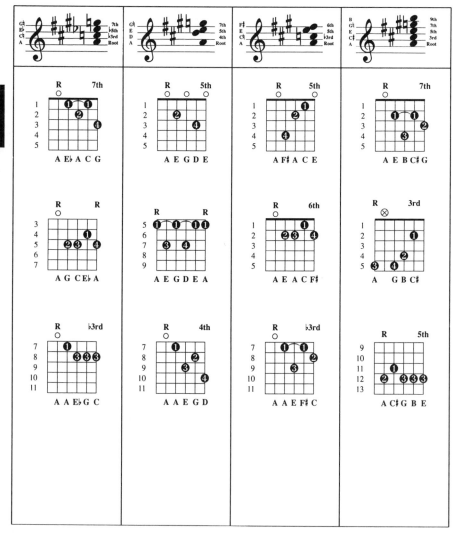

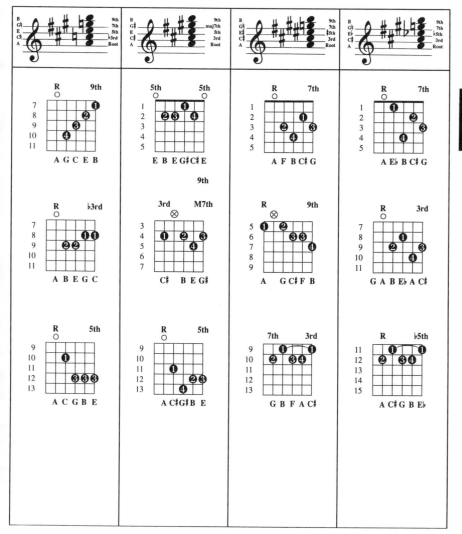

73

A7-9   A7#9   A6 9   A11

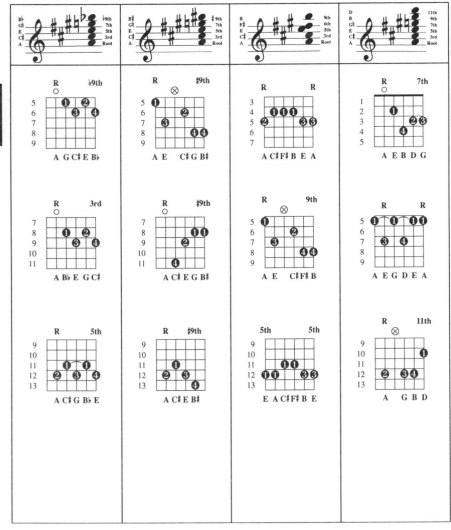

A7-9

R   ♭9th
5 ❶ ❷
6   ❸ ❹
7
8
9
A G C♯ E B♭

R   3rd
7 ❶ ❷
8
9   ❸ ❹
10
11
A B♭ E G C♯

R   5th
9
10
11 ❶ ❶
12 ❷ ❸ ❹
13
A C♯ G B♭ E

A7#9

R   #9th
⊗
5 ❶
6   ❷
7 ❸
8   ❹❹
9
A E C♯ G B♯

R   #9th
○
7 ❶❶
8
9   ❷
10
11 ❹
A C♯ E G B♯

R   #9th
9
10
11 ❶
12 ❷ ❸
13   ❹
A C♯ E B♯

A6 9

R   R
3
4 ❶❶❶
5 ❷   ❸❸
6
7
A C♯ F♯ B E A

R   9th
⊗
5 ❶
6   ❷
7 ❸
8   ❹❹
9
A E C♯ F♯ B

5th   5th
9
10
11 ❶❶
12 ❶❶   ❸❸
13
E A C♯ F♯ B E

A11

R   7th
○
1
2 ❶
3   ❷❸
4   ❹
5
A E B D G

R   R
5 ❶ ❶ ❶❶
6
7 ❸ ❹
8
9
A E G D E A

R   11th
⊗
9
10   ❶
11
12 ❷ ❸❹
13
A   G B D

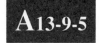

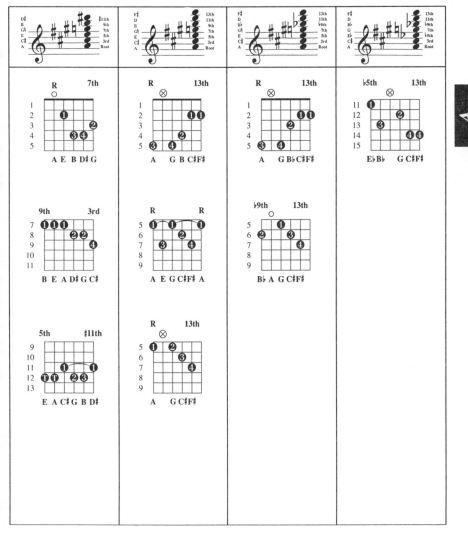

Key of:

B♭

B♭   **B♭m**   **B♭7**

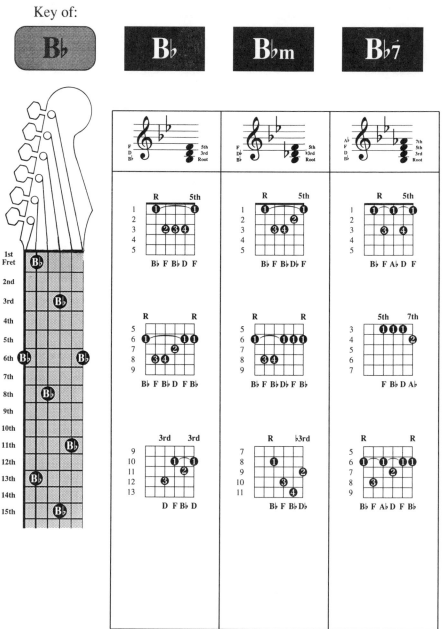

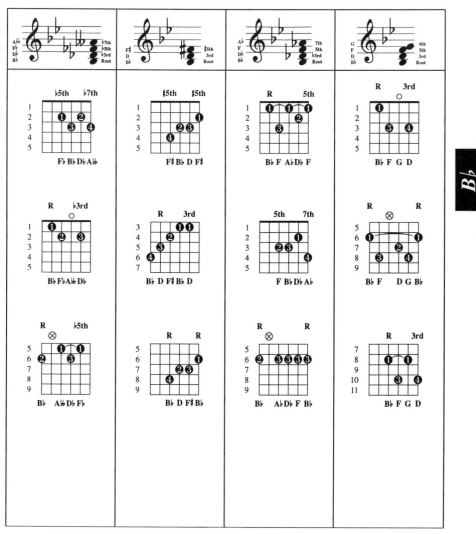

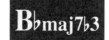

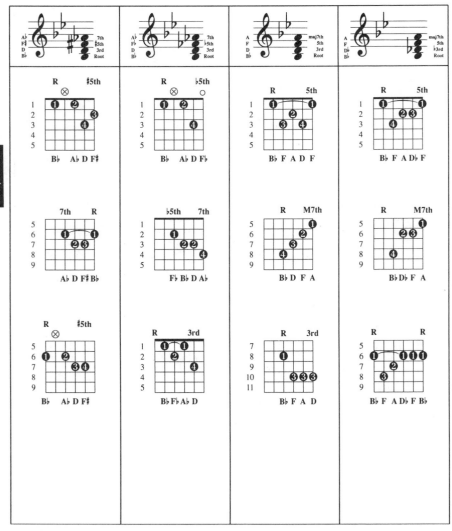

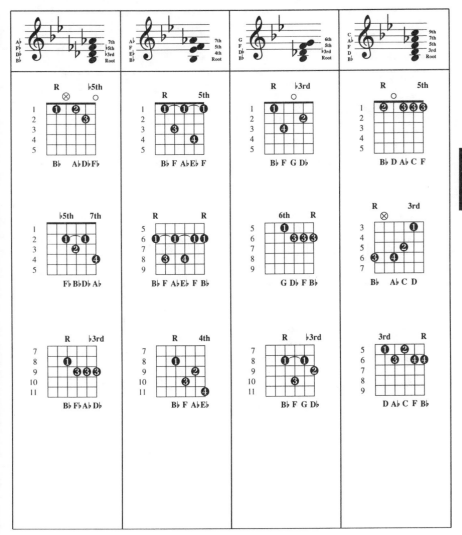

79

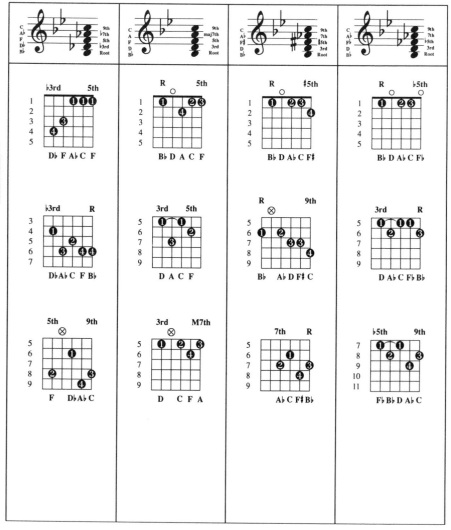

80

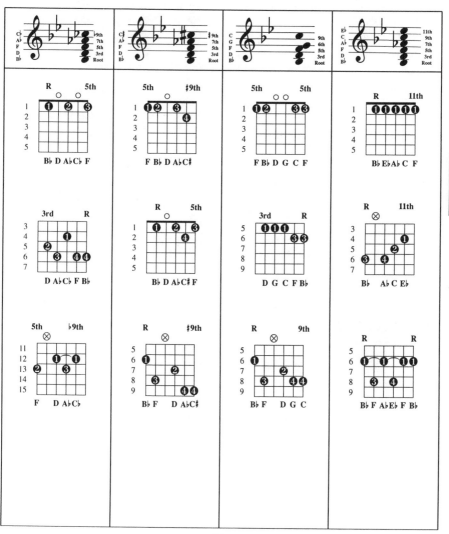

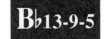

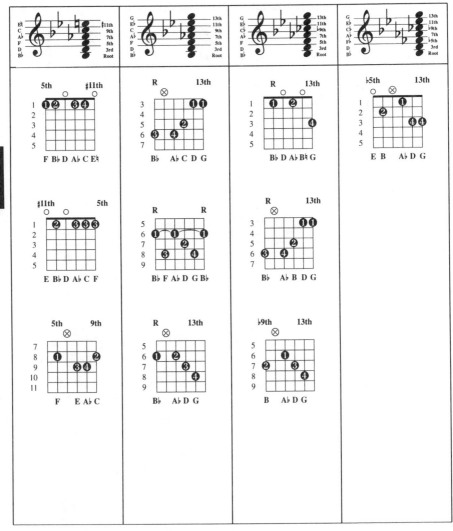

82

Key of:

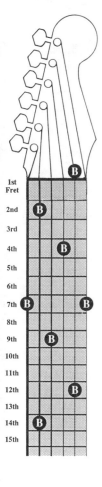

1st Fret
2nd
3rd
4th
5th
6th
7th
8th
9th
10th
11th
12th
13th
14th
15th

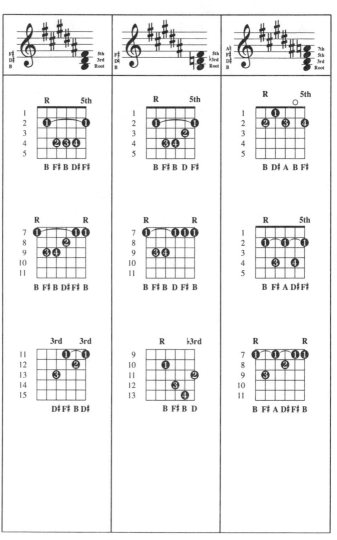

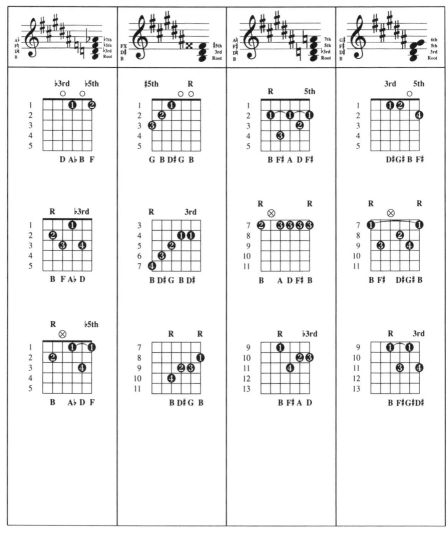

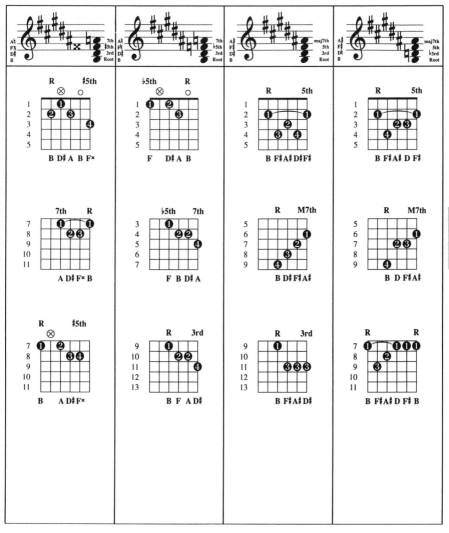

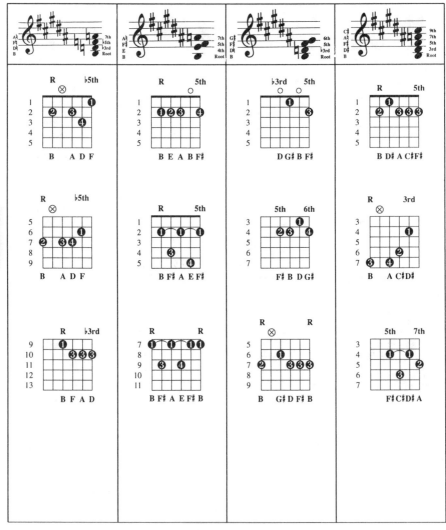

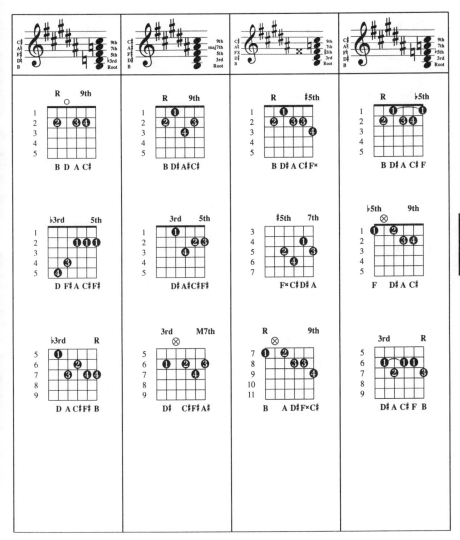

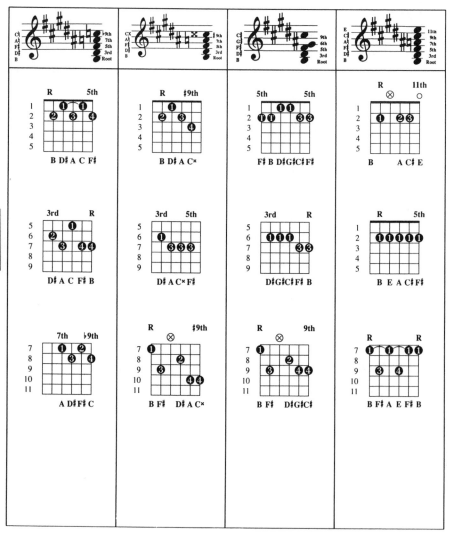

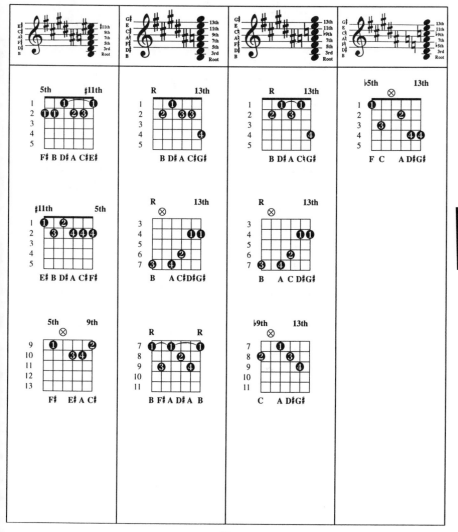

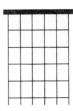
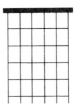
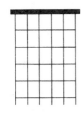
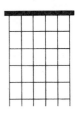
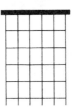
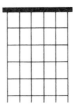
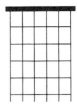
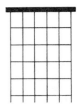
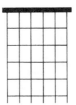
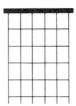
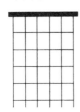
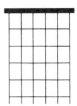
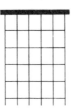

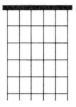

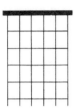
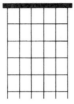

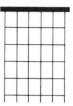
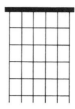
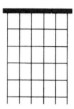
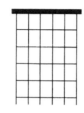
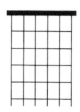
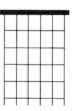

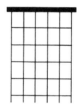
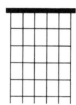
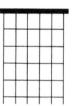
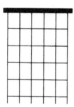
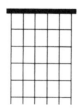
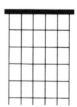
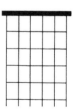

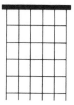

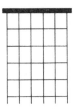
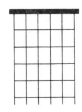
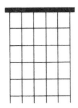
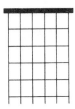
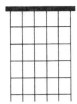
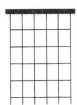
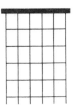
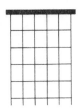
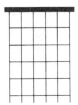
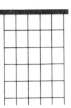

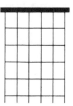
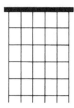
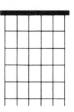

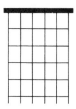
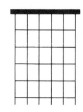
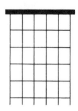

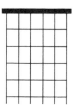
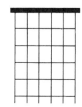
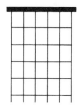

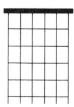
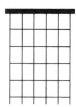
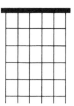

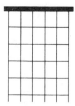
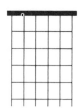
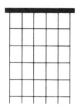
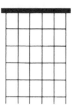